An Intentional Home

Creating Spaces for Living Beautifully

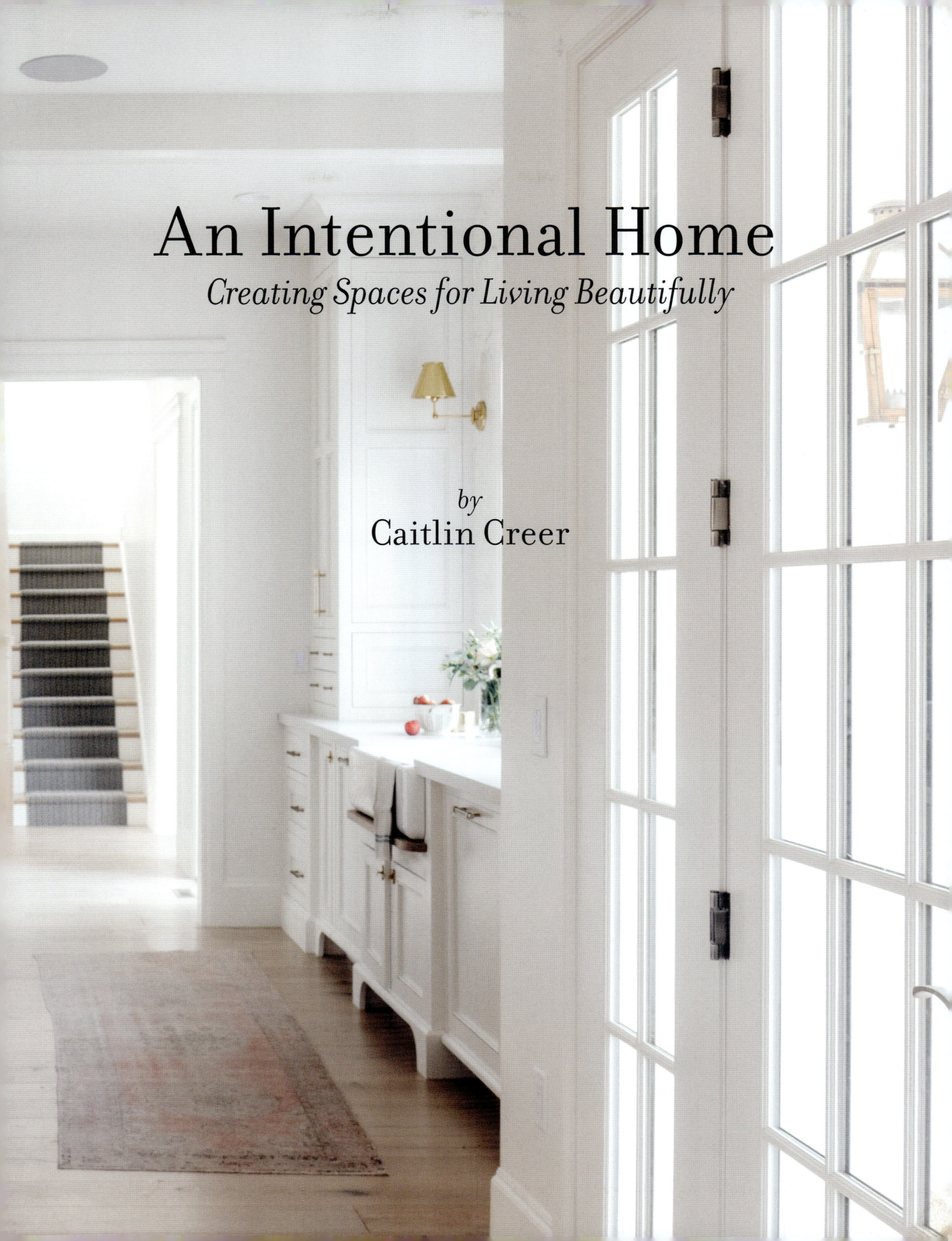

An Intentional Home

Creating Spaces for Living Beautifully

by

Caitlin Creer

ISBN: 979-8-9882362-3-8

Library of Congress Control Number: 2024937968

Book Cover and Interior Design: Brooke Williams
Cover Photography: Julia D'Agostino (front cover), Lindsey Stewart (back cover)
Interior Photography: Julia D'Agostino, Lindsey Stewart, and Rebekah Westover
Writer: Britney Mellen
Copyeditor: Catherine Pavia

Printed in China

10 9 8 7 6 5 4 3 2 1

First Edition: October 2024

Jumelle Press
3350 S. 2940 E. #9690
Salt Lake City, UT 84109
www.jumellepress.com
@jumellepress

To my family, you are the best thing I have helped to create.
Home is wherever I'm with you.

Contents

Foreword

by Paloma Contreras

Life has a funny way of coming full circle when you least expect it. I got my start in the design industry when I began writing my former blog, *La Dolce Vita*, in July 2007. The blog set me on the path towards my destiny as an interior designer, with a few stops along the winding way. My blog gave me a voice; it allowed me to tap into my true passion; and it helped me to find my purpose in life. It connected me with countless wonderful and inspiring people, including many who became friends or even mentors. It gave me a foundation on which to build a business that would eventually include owning a retail store and becoming an author.

What you may not know is that while I was still a creatively stifled high school Spanish teacher, Caitlin's blog was among the very first I ever read. I found her through a mutual friend that I had gone to high school with. Caitlin and my high school friend became acquainted while living in New York where Caitlin had already begun tapping into her love of design, which she shared on her blog. Inspired and desperately in need of a creative outlet to soften the sting of a career that just didn't fit, I decided that I, too, could do "that." By "that," I meant writing a blog. After all, I'd always enjoyed writing and it seemed like a great outlet for my random musings. This was in the very earliest days of blogging and none of us knew the power this new platform held. When my husband and I purchased our first house, my blog began to organically take on more of a design focus, and eventually, people took notice. The rest, as they say, is history! Thank you, Caitlin, for introducing me to the world of blogs and for nudging me towards what would become an extraordinary path, even if you did not realize it at the time.

Caitlin's own design journey has been remarkable to watch. Eventually, she and her young family moved back to Utah where she built an amazing business as both an interior designer and shop owner. While her days may be busier, one thing has remained the same over the years—Caitlin's timeless, classic American style. Reflected throughout the projects featured in the pages of this book, Caitlin's work is at once elegant and effortless. There is something about the soothing color palettes she uses that make the viewer want to take a relaxing deep breath. Designing spaces that make people feel at ease is no easy feat, but fear not: Caitlin will walk you through her design process through every page of *An Intentional Home*.

"Reflected throughout the projects featured in the pages of this book, Caitlin's work is at once elegant and effortless."

Every year when January 1 rolls around, rather than set resolutions, I set intentions. There is something a bit gentler and more open-minded about that approach versus declaring that you are going to give up sweets or exercise every day, only to fail two days into the New Year. This more philosophical approach has worked for me for a long time, so I was delighted to learn that Caitlin begins her design projects by setting intentions with her clients. There is something so beautiful about entering the designer-client relationship as partners with true intentions to craft a meaningful home together. If you are embarking on your design project on your own, know that you have a partner in Caitlin, who lays it all out so beautifully and intentionally throughout the pages of this wonderful book.

Paloma Contreras

Introduction

I love having a designated spot in my home to start my day. I pull back the linen drapes in our formal living room to let in the early morning light, and with a cup of rosehip tea and a crackling fire, I settle into my deep-seated sofa and get a head start on my to-do list. One morning I might send a follow-up email to an architect, put the final touches on a client's room plan, and finalize a collection for my store, while the next morning I might get on a conference call with a client and contractor on the East Coast. Balancing my nationwide design business with a retail store and website is no small task as a mom of five, so I love these quiet moments before the pitter patter of tiny feet begin to make their way down the stairs. I designed this room intentionally to support me in these quiet hours, with task lighting, handy surfaces on which to set a teacup or a laptop, and a woolen cream-colored throw draped over the sofa. I also designed this room to support moments with my children; after all, they do eventually make it down the stairs!

My very first conversation with a new client is a discussion about intentions: What speaks to you? How do you want your home to feel? What moments do you want to experience in your home? Intentionally creating spaces to support those endeavors is the heart of my philosophy. In this book I will take you through each step of mindfully selecting every option for your home with an end in mind. If you aren't sure about the end yet, I'll help you discover that, too.

Take a step into any of my projects and what sets the space apart is not necessarily the hand-carved millwork or bespoke throw pillows (although those certainly make an impact). What makes a home feel special—at any size or budget—is the intentionality behind what we have selected and the story we are telling. In my experience, I have found that people begin "imagining home" long before they actually set out to create a home of their own. It may only be glimpses, but I have seen how clarity about the way we want to live can come to us in fleeting moments or experiences. It can come to us in color palettes, textures, materials, or specific items—even places. You may not realize it, but you've likely been collecting pieces along the way, and I will help you, just as I help my clients, stitch all of those together to create a home.

I recently traveled to Ireland with a group of other architects, designers, and builders to explore the rich history and beautiful landscape. I tend to be someone who veers toward a light and

"At times the scales may tip toward the form or toward the function, but maintaining that sense of intention is what creates a beautiful and livable home."

fresh aesthetic, so I was delighted—and a little surprised—to discover how captivated I was with the rich woods, delicate carving, stonework, and heavy velvets and tweeds. They felt comforting to me, and I was inspired to find ways to bring this storied look to my own home. This doesn't necessarily mean I'm lining my walls with mahogany paneling or hanging a family crest, but it did push me to expand my limits of how and where I incorporate deeper and richer colors and materials into my designs. This may translate as a herringbone blanket, a velvet piece of upholstery, or an antique piece with years of patina. What makes our spaces and our lives interesting is how we choose to integrate what speaks to us.

You are the authority on how you want to live, and it is within your power to create a home that supports you. I wish I had the bandwidth to embrace every project that comes my way, but I have intentionally kept a rotating roster of select projects that is manageable by my small team and me. This book is an invitation to use what I've learned in my years of experience to help you explore what resonates with you and to know how to integrate it into your life and home.

Creating a home is as much about the books on our shelves and the art on our walls as it is about the architecture and finishes. There is an art to crafting the details around us and true creativity is reinventing familiar concepts in novel or unexpected ways. When we find that intersection of what makes sense for our lives and what is appealing to the eye, we've created something special. At times the scales may tip toward the form or toward the function but, maintaining that sense of intention is what creates a beautiful and livable home. Let's create yours.

Caitlin Creer

1

Reflect

Notice the places and spaces
that speak to you

Growing up, I had a friend whose home felt magical. I can still envision the mature garden and the way the ivy climbed the front gable. Inside, an impressive two-story formal room featured a delicate iron staircase, below which sat a beautiful baby grand piano. It clearly wasn't a room intended for teenagers, but whenever we lounged in there, I was transported. Each tabletop boasted a splendid collection of relics: interesting coffee table books and antique magnifying glasses with dainty mother of pearl handles, complemented by elegant silk curtains and sumptuous upholstery. I studied each detail with dedicated awe, as if in a museum. The curated, artful display and sophistication clearly resonated with me on a deeper level than I could articulate at the time and has become a part of me.

What has become a part of you? Where have you been? What do you love? These are some of the questions I ask new clients as we develop a "home DNA" that resonates with their perceptions of what a home should be and how it should feel. As you ask yourself these same questions, remember that there is no right answer: the answers are as varied as there are people. Memorable life experiences, places you have lived or traveled, and cultural influences you are drawn to can all be alchemized into a vision of home that is uniquely your own. The first step is to take note of what you love and why you love it.

From an early age I always loved things pertaining to home. As a child, I spent hours crafting elaborately decorated apartment buildings for my dolls in a bookshelf. I enjoyed setting up more than actually playing! It's no wonder I observed my friend's welcoming home with such delight—it felt like a life-size manifestation of my imagination. As I grew, so did my canvas as I continued to expand my ideas about home and living. What started out as experiments in a dollhouse became a love of art and architecture and eventually a career in home design.

Through the years, a constant source of inspiration for me has been places in which I have lived and traveled—Florence, Rosemary Beach, and, of course, New York City, one of my favorites. The juxtaposition of historic brick buildings with modern finishes, converted lofts, and the creative energy and culture in New York keep me eagerly exploring. There is always a new layer of

This generational ranch, inspired by early twentieth century lodges, was created for families to gather. We added a sense of history through layers: oil paintings evoke the rich colors of the landscape, pillow textiles reference the sturdy denim of a barn jacket, and sheepskin adds a note of warmth to the space.

inspiration to be discovered, from an interesting tile pattern in a subterranean subway station to an astonishing chandelier in the tallest skyscraper.

One of my favorite places to visit in the city is the Astor Chinese Garden Court inside the Metropolitan Museum of Art. This special spot taught me about the transformative power of an intentionally designed space. Amid a bustling city, visitors are transported to a traditional Chinese garden with meandering tile paths, rock compositions, and the sound of gently trickling water. I've visited many times to clear my mind and get a dose of peace and quiet in my day.

I also love to spend hours wandering the luxurious department stores and boutiques in the city. The preppy plaids and antique oil paintings at Ralph Lauren have made their way into my heart, along with the globally curated displays and artisanal wares at ABC Carpet & Home. I marvel at how these dynamic collections of textiles and color can take me from Upper East Side luxury to a vibrant, bohemian market within a few subway stops. From these visits, I gained an understanding for how an intentionally curated space can tell a story and create an experience.

When my studies took me abroad to Europe, I discovered some of my favorite artists. Known as the "Monet of Spain," Joaquin Sorolla's impressionist seascapes filled my mind with the beauty of nature and calming, coastal colors which have become a palette of choice. Throughout my studies, I developed an appreciation for complementary color schemes; thoughtful composition; and the use of emotion, history, and place; all concepts that come together to create a cohesive outcome, be it a work of art or a room.

All of these influences have become a part of my own ethos, a strong, traditional foundation infused with a love of casual living. Sometimes fancy but never fussy, always welcoming and thoroughly livable. The strands that make up one's style and home DNA come from diverse lived experiences, inspirations, and aspirations. If I've done my job, no two projects I work on have the same genetic makeup and your home is no exception. While projects may share similar threads, I always strive to make sure there is an authentic signature that sets each home apart. After you reflect on your life experiences, favorite places, and influences, you are ready to distill your unique point of view into a vision of home.

This light-flooded, upper level kids lounge, is positioned right off the children's bedrooms and is an ideal spot for reading, relaxing, and playing games with family and friends.

OPPOSITE The best vignettes are personal and memorable. This console and scalloped chair were both purchased through an estate sale at the former home of Susie Hilfiger. The paintings above were commissioned by our client to remember a family vacation. **ABOVE LEFT** In my home I intentionally surround myself with things I love: books from my childhood, a candle purchased in Italy, and an antique painting, reminiscent of an idyllic childhood summer. **ABOVE RIGHT** On this raw wood table, I display a cherished photo of my two daughters, a brass container from my mother, and a pine cone foraged from a trip to Ireland.

STEVEN GAMBREL
PERSPECTIVE

ABOVE This corner embraces the interplay of pattern, color, and texture. These floral and check cottage elements feel collected and historic. **OPPOSITE** The atmosphere in this airy guest room is feminine and magical. Affectionately referred to as "The Sisters' Room", it was designed specifically for the client's sisters who often visit.

While this room might read "formal," the durable fabric and deep cushions create a casual family gathering space, perfect for after-school reading and lively conversations. From custom shades of periwinkle blue and blush pink to the antique Italian gilt candlesticks, this room represents a convergence of this client's tastes and interests.

OPPOSITE These doors selected by the client were one of the original anchors that set the tone for this home. **ABOVE** An entry is a chance to create a feeling of welcome and to infuse personality into the home. Inspired by a favorite hotel, The Mayflower Inn & Spa in Connecticut, we incorporated an olive tree as a statement element.

BELOW Our client wanted to incorporate a personal, hotel-like experience into their everyday routine. This translated into antique bathroom accessories, a place to display meaningful perfumes, and custom monogrammed shades. **OPPOSITE** In a luxe ground floor bathroom, we added interest via the fabric on the drapery and stool.

Surround yourself with things you love deeply—that take you to visit favorite moments in your life.

Koichi Takada

A perfectly appointed cozy cabin weaves together a nostalgic vision the client had for a space that feels "old" but functions with all the modern amenities of a new home.

OPPOSITE Reclaimed beams establish the character of this refined ranch. With a specific spectrum of color in mind, I selected each from a snowy Midwest lumber yard. **ABOVE (TOP)** We created a station for a client who cherishes the tranquil ritual of teatime. **ABOVE (BOTTOM)** For homes situated in beautiful, wild landscapes, we often build rooms to make the views part of the interior experience.

OPPOSITE Some spaces in our homes are designed to create a moment of serenity. I love how this space evokes feelings of sun on your face and a soft breeze. **ABOVE** As a former New Yorker, I fell in love with this capture of a bustling Grand Central Station by artist Paul Ferney. It sparks joy whenever I walk past it.

This client desired a casual, coastal atmosphere for this family room. Deep, comfortably upholstered furniture in durable fabrics can withstand spills and accommodate afternoon naps for this family's tall teenage boys. Wicker, pale wood, and blue linen textures create a sense of calm.

This gathering space is intimate enough to hang out in as a family, yet expansive enough to host events. We achieved this duality with high ceilings and intimate seating arrangements.

2

Envision

Develop a vision of home that
is uniquely your own

Now is the time to develop a mood board, where intangible images, ideas, and words meet actual materials, colors, and swatches. Several years ago, a client walked into one of our design meetings carrying a basket of freshly laid eggs from her chicken coop. The soft blue, cafe au lait, and springy green eggs encapsulated her idea of how she wanted her home to feel: warm, welcoming, and familiar. Right then and there, we determined that we would use this pastoral palette as a foundation for our vision; if any of our choices veered too far from our earthy inspiration, this little basket would guide us back to the feeling we were trying to create.

How do you want your home to feel? More specifically, how do you want to feel in your home? Your answers to these questions can help you develop your vision from a personal, internal place, recalling the images and memories you conjured in the last chapter. Reflect on those feelings. Envision how you might bring those to life in your own home. One client found inspiration for her restrained farmhouse from Norwegian landscapes and chunky knits. A mood board for the study of another client included an image of an English library and swatches of tanned leather and hardy woolen plaids. Whether you pull together ideas physically or digitally, your mood board will help guide your decisions going forward and will ultimately lead to a home that supports the life you want to live.

I have learned over the years that when people lean into their own authenticity to create something original, the magic begins. Bring all your inspiration to the table to reveal the unique mix of influences that will help define your home's specific vibe and identity. You might love mid-century furnishings but have a penchant for romantic florals. Or maybe you love rustic, mountain living but you live in a downtown apartment. The juxtaposition of different eras, styles, and influences is what creates that indefinable mix that can be summed up by one word and one aesthetic—yours.

Once a particularly endearing client walked into her finished home at the end of our installation, and although we had been working closely together for several years, she still looked around with wonder and said with astonishment, "It's like I walked into my own mind!" We had worked intentionally to combine her traditional roots with her passion for curated antiques and whim-

This lakeside lodge was envisioned as a long-term gathering spot for these outdoor-enthusiast clients. A pair of snowshoes set casually atop an antique Belgian cabinet compliments the beautiful reclaimed wood ceiling and infuses a sense of history into the new build.

sical color, indeed capturing the perfect blend. The goal was not to replicate a specific look, but to create a home that felt like an expression of her imagination in a gratifying and personal way.

As your vision takes shape, you will want to define the colors that will reinforce the feeling you want to create. When determining a color palette for a home, I first like to define a range of colors to work within. Study your inspiration images to determine what colors you see. Are we working within the extremes of black and white or a softer charcoal and warm cream? Are we leaning towards neutrals or vibrant shades? Do we want to evoke something specific? Because our egg-inspired palette felt very springy and fresh, very bright or dark colors would not have felt right. By identifying and defining a curated spectrum to pull from, you'll have a framework to guide decisions going forward. By staying within this framework, you needn't worry if things "match"—aim to keep things complimentary, which is always more interesting and timeless.

Drawing on your inspiration pictures, identify what motifs and materials reinforce your vision. Different types of wood, metal finishes, stone, and tile can come together in entirely unique ways for vastly different outcomes. Italian marble, deep patinas, and sumptuous velvets feel utterly posh and moody, while crisp white cabinetry, leaded glass, and polished nickel transport me to a coastal, cottage kitchen. I've found the sum is always greater than the parts. It still thrills me to see details come together.

Developing a vision is always my favorite part of the design process. There is something empowering about turning intangible thoughts and ideas into a physical space; it is not just an exercise in aesthetics but a path towards the life you want to live. From a stack of magazine pages or bookmarked digital images to an heirloom art piece or swatch of vintage floral brocade, if it evokes a feeling in you, it belongs on your mood board. Save, print, or pin your favorites and begin to define a home where they belong.

CABIN STYLE

OPPOSITE Our client envisioned a space in her kitchen where she could prepare meals while having conversations with her teenagers, so we prioritized a wide countertop and comfortable stools. **BELOW** Inspired by nostalgic cabins, we wrapped the walls in reclaimed wood to create an inviting reading nook.

This home is designed to accommodate the client's large family. Essential to creating an entertaining space are comfortable upholstery, an easy flow, and room to expand.

This restrained primary bath is elevated enough to feel special, but maintains the same tone-downed formality as the rest of the house.

BELOW This light-filled hallway avoids being sterile with the addition of a beautiful wood ceiling and wool rugs. **OPPOSITE** Guided by the vision of chunky woolen knits and views of the breathtaking mountain landscape beyond, an air of laid-back luxury infuses this cabin.

As a central point in this home, we envisioned a space that would present well for parties, but could also endure the daily wear and tear of children and teenagers.

The true secret of happiness
lies in taking a genuine interest
in the details of daily life.

William Morris

This client envisioned a sense of unity among the varied bedrooms on the second floor. To achieve this, we included a layer of this pretty powder blue color in each space.

Our approach is to design the foundational elements, in this case the stunning cabinetry, and then integrate layers to tell the story of the home. All the extra details—lighting, art, furnishings, and the collected but functional kitchen pieces—reflect the specific personality of this home and client.

Cannelle et Vanille
LET ME FEED YOU Rosie Daykin

Whether the vision for a home is broad or specific, it is often the subtle details, such as a brass trim or scallop accent, that transform a room from generic to personal.

Elements of wicker and wood are integrated throughout this family home, from the curved shaped sconces in a cozy attic window seat, to baskets in the family room, corralling toys and books. We like to incorporate wicker in homes to ground a space and add a natural element.

OPPOSITE While the feeling in this primary suite is serene and the overall aesthetic traditional, abstract art by Brooklyn Day creates energy and interest. **ABOVE LEFT** The vision for a space can be as much about what you don't see as what you do see. Early on in the design process we allocate not only the visual ideas, but also the functional storage. **ABOVE RIGHT** Authentic materials like stone, metal, and wood provide a sense of character and timelessness that manufactured materials cannot replicate.

I don't know if we have ever designed a room that was as specific and personal as this office library. Following a moodboard of tweeds and old English libraries, we painstakingly adjusted these cabinets to ensure the height and depth would be ideal for this treasured book collection. Over the fireplace is a vintage painting of New York where the homeowner used to live.

SOUTH AFRICA
TITAN

3

Define

Invite intentional, elevated moments into every day

When I think of moments in my own home, most of them are centered around my children. At any given moment of the day, a child is likely climbing onto an available lap, leaning on a shoulder, or plopping down to have a quick chat. It should come as no surprise that my house is designed for snuggling. There are welcoming places to sit and lounge in almost every room. There are nubby, linen throw blankets draped over chairs and tucked into wicker baskets. There are French candles for ambiance and plump, down pillows for comfort. This isn't by chance. We have intentionally created spaces to relax, connect, and be cozy.

Whatever your aspirations for your home, think about what kinds of supportive spaces are essential for those experiences. Then, identify where you want them to be. By taking a thoughtful analysis of how you want to live, you identify your higher ideals. You can envision how the home will be a backdrop for your life and you can define spaces that are value-driven in form and function. What moments do you want to create in your home and why?

Everyone requires different things from a home. Maybe you love to entertain and long for welcoming spaces to gather. Perhaps you are an early riser and dream of that spot to plan your day or enjoy your coffee. For my family of seven, I imagine a large, weathered kitchen table for birthday cakes, long Sunday dinners, and enough space for the kids to spread out their school and art projects.

I have a client who loves to host large gatherings at her home, from book groups and musical performances to charity events and family reunions. With a lot of people comes a lot of outerwear (especially during chilly New England winters), so we designed a thoughtful coat room for visitors. We curated a small, charming space with low, flattering lighting, gorgeous floral wallpaper, and sturdy, strategically placed hooks dotting the wall. A mirror and a bowl of breath mints on an antique occasional table completes the vignette. The act of hanging a coat becomes a delightful moment for family and friends.

My favorite room in my own home is a large living room with windows on three sides and a charming marble fireplace. It is right off our entry, bathed in sunlight for most of the day because

This moody formal living room is a study in light and dark. Defined as a more sophisticated space, curated antiques give it an aged, traditional aesthetic, while the evergreen sofa showcases the client's personality. The juxtaposition of different elements makes this room feel both collected and inviting.

of the placement of the windows. I wanted this room to support cozy moments with my family and my own morning rituals. We debated over whether to include a television and ultimately decided to put it in the basement family room. Even without electronics, everyone is drawn to the warmth of this room, full of sunshine and comfy blankets, making it ideal for taking respite in a sunny corner, reading, talking, and gathering. I value these fleeting moments with my children and this room ensures they happen often.

Another thing I value is spontaneous entertaining. So many things in life are planned, but I've found some of my favorite memories and gatherings happen spontaneously. A neighbor swings by last-minute, the kids show up with a group of friends, family members drop in to watch a football game (that's when the basement TV comes in handy, along with an enormous sectional and piles of pillows!). I love inviting an unexpected visitor to enjoy a cup of tea or a slice of cake at the kitchen counter, conveying the message that they are welcome to linger. Impromptu events can be memorable and an easy "yes" with minimal preparation. For my life, being casually prepared looks like a well-stocked fridge, fresh flowers on the table, plenty of (clean!) plates at the ready, and an open door.

Life moves so quickly with places to be and things to do that I savor these moments at home. Taking the time to define your desired experiences gives you design direction as you begin to intentionally select items that will go in each room. As you stay mindful of what is important and how you want to live, you are empowered to create rooms where form and function come together to support and elevate every moment.

BELOW The charm of this butler's pantry is a result of the striking chinoiserie wallpaper, dramatic brass sink, and delicate collection of antique mirrors. **OPPOSITE** Identical baskets keep less frequently used items concealed but accessible.

BREAD

Having worked with this client on a previous mudroom, we had a head start on designing this well-organized, hard-working space. In addition to an antique bench and bespoke cabinetry, a vintage painting reminiscent of the client's three children is hung on the back wall.

OPPOSITE Defined by an antique travertine table and pair of skirted linen chairs, this elegant, multi-purpose laundry room is equipped for a variety of tasks, from wrapping gifts to folding clothes. **ABOVE** Our client treasures this inherited heirloom desk. After a careful restoration it now resides in an upstairs guest room.

The dialogue between client and architect is about as intimate as any conversation you can have, because, when you're talking about building a house, you're talking about dreams.

Robert A. M. Stern

For clients who love to entertain, this pantry, tucked behind an equally stunning kitchen, is an ideal place to party prep, hide a mess, and contain the overflow when needed.

OPPOSITE We designed this back mudroom to provide storage for all the hats, coats, shoes, and extras of this busy family of six. **ABOVE** This bench can travel easily from a mudroom landing spot to become extra seating in a family room.

Regardless of the function of a room, we always aim to include an extra spot to sit, whether for a peaceful moment, or as part of a daily routine.

Our client requested two features in their gourmet kitchen: an artful slab for the island and a statement La Cornue range. Working harmoniously together, they anchor this beautiful kitchen.

BELOW When designing a home, a request to "contain the clutter" is often at the top of a family's priority list. In this work space, eggshell blue cabinetry conceals office supplies while a pinboard corrals loose papers. **OPPOSITE** In this den, necessities like toys and blankets are carefully housed in built-in lower cabinets.

Pacific Natural
AT HOME
JAKE ARNOLD
MISSISSIPPI BLOOD
Reunion
Nelson DeMille
C.S. Lewis
INTERNATIONAL COOK BOOK
MADE FOR LIVING
SCOTT SHRADER THE ART OF OUTDOOR LIVING
ART TREASURES OF THE LOUVRE

OPPOSITE Most rooms can benefit from incorporating a cozy spot. This chaise, upholstered in an interesting yet subtle pattern, is the most-loved space in this primary bedroom. **BELOW** Designed for lounging, this seating area includes a deep-seated sofa and a sturdy table for snacks or games.

BELOW When designing a space, I love to imagine not only the whole room, but even the details of intimate corners. **OPPOSITE** After spotting these Burleigh plates on a trip to England, the client asked us to incorporate them in a thoughtful way.

THE SILVER SPOON CLASSIC
KINFOLK

4

Create

Make a plan and
bring your vision to life

After reflecting on what inspires you, envisioning how you want your home to feel, and defining the moments you want to enjoy, it's time to turn all of those ideas into actual home details. Create a strong foundation with a smart floor plan, thoughtful selection of design elements, and smart storage. Begin by asking yourself one question: Who lives here? After all, without the people who bring it to life, a home is just a structure. The distinct personalities and lives of your home's inhabitants should inform every decision you make, taking into account past experiences and future possibilities. A well-curated home is both biographical and aspirational, and I believe it is at this critical juncture where the choices you make can support the entire journey.

Before we consider any individual pieces of furniture, we assess the flow, the fit, and the function of different layouts. A grand hall for entertaining and hosting will be arranged differently than a small den for reading and studying. One musical client dreamt of a space that could adapt quickly for everything from close gatherings by the fireplace to large piano concerts—and even a Mariachi band! We were able to create a feeling of intimacy even in a grand hall (complete with 20-foot sloped ceilings), using generous hand-knotted wool rugs, small groupings of sumptuously upholstered pieces, and a fireplace and grand piano to anchor the space. By creating smaller arrangements, we created rooms within a room, adding cohesive design elements to unify the space.

The elements that make up a thoughtful design are similar to ingredients in a recipe; we introduce different flavors to get a desired look and feel. In one inviting mountain retreat among aspens and pines, we wanted the finished home to capture a rustic lifestyle in a refined way. Reclaimed oak beams, floors, and paneling brought a sense of history and warmth, which we augmented with artisan, hand-painted tiles, and forged iron lighting. Woven seating, worn leather, and antique rugs added yet another warm layer to this idyllic homestead. Any of these design elements could be applied individually to a variety of projects, but this unique mix of elements gave this home its distinct flavor.

Creative ideas can be integrated in many forms. One unexpected detail for a client's design came while working on a home in Midway, Utah, a small Swiss-influenced mountain village. The

When imagining homes for clients, I always strive to make room for "more". This applies nicely to storage, seating, chairs at the dinner table, and in this case, places to sleep.

client valued keeping the home anchored in its bucolic surroundings, but was open to innovation, including an idea from our ingenious cabinetmaker, who had seen an interesting detail in a Nordic castle. We incorporated this profile into a bracket for the floating wood shelving that flanked the tumbled stone fireplace, translating this unexpected inspiration into something tangible with a unique detail that enhanced the individuality of the home.

Finally, a plan for organization is a must. When building or renovating, custom carpentry and cabinetry are a wonderful way to enhance the aesthetics and functionality of a room, but the right stand-alone pieces will also work. I love to implement an abundance of specific storage in every place possible: custom-built bunk rooms for cousins and grandkids (especially in vacation homes), pool lockers, craft desks, and, of course, kitchens, laundry rooms, and other utility spaces. One in particular comes to mind: the client had a beloved French bulldog named Bleu, the unofficial mascot of the home (whose owner also fittingly loves the color blue). They needed a landing spot for sweet Bleu and a place to corral all the pet accoutrements. We jumped at the opportunity to add a built-in kennel with a brass ventilated panel, storage for grooming necessities, and a convenient spot for food and treats, all in a soothing shade of cornflower blue.

As you create a plan for each room, all those ideas that have been floating around become something real. This is when the initial vision becomes joint property of all who live in the home. Although my design team and I manage our projects to get to a spectacularly "finished" state, the truth is that a home is not a static thing. Just like the people who live there, it will always be evolving and developing. Set your home up for success by creating a solid foundation to stand the test of time, and it will support you through changing seasons and stages of life.

Designed for the client's many nieces and nephews, this meticulously designed, carefully constructed, space is a happy retreat for sleepovers with visiting cousins and friends. A memorable, bright bunk room is truly what childhood dreams are made of.

PRADA
CHANEL

"Dream closet" doesn't quite describe this space. Darling knobs were the perfect discovery for our bow-loving client while the island has become a personal curation of beloved items.

This jewel box office provides a tiny sanctuary for our client. Adjoining cabinetry was thoughtfully designed to support the logistics of daily function while maintaining the serene atmosphere evoked by the whimsical wallpaper.

We call this space "Grandma's attic." Its charming and eclectic mix is intended to feel collected even though this space was newly furnished.

BELOW A single chair is a great way to anchor a small space. The striped chair in this charming foyer serves as a landing spot for this attic guest suite. **OPPOSITE** In this studious child's room, we created a space for him to draw and write to his heart's content.

Everything I've done is about life and how people live and how they want to live and how they dream they'll live. That's what I do.

Ralph Lauren

Brass pendants, seagrass counter stools, and skylights define this classic space. In a back hallway, we incorporated crisp white molding and brass hooks beneath an earthy linen stripe wallpaper to echo this home's neutral cottage aesthetic.

OPPOSITE We envisioned this dry bar as a space that could be functional storage and a collected display of our client's favorite things. **ABOVE** In the adjoining family room, a blush linen ottoman and carefully selected art books continue the ethereal color palette.

OPPOSITE Using baskets on high shelves is an ideal way to rotate seasonal items and break up large spans of cabinetry. **BELOW** We thoughtfully considered the best way to integrate this window seat to capture an upstairs view while also providing much-needed storage.

Good design is often created through strategic layering and an exchange between materials. An unlacquered brass faucet shines against the clean simplicity of the soapstone counters; this range's green paint highlights the adjoining metal panels; the golden tones in this quartzite slab are enhanced by the white oak cabinetry below.

This finished space would feel so different without the interest added by the understated backsplash tile. It instantly grounds the space.

BAIES
SUNDAY SUPPERS

History of Art
Ballet
Henry Leutwyler

5

Establish

Choose pieces that will
stand the test of time

From our early apartments to our home today with five children, we have moved many times. With each move, I carefully assessed what we would need to feel settled and functional in a new space, establishing a home wherever we were. As a newlywed armed with a stack of gift cards, some paint brushes, and a keen eye at my local vintage and consignment stores (and maybe a garage sale or two), I was determined to outfit each home in a way that felt intentional and well designed. In fact, you might say I was my own first client.

I collected pieces for our first apartment that felt like they would be a good foundation and give us longevity with their classic design, history, and versatility; a taupe canvas sofa, a wood heirloom desk from my husband's childhood bedroom, and a solid round dining table that I rescued from a donation pile, all finished off with a collection of black and white photos, simply framed. Living in small apartments taught me that every item I brought home needed to earn its keep, and I am still ruthless about making sure every item in a home is not only pretty but purposeful. What pieces do you need to accomplish your goals? Whether starting at square one or refreshing an existing space, I think the lessons I learned in those early years still apply.

I have worked on hundreds of homes, with a range of needs and budgets, and I always come back to the importance of committing to long-term pieces. We live in an era where it's tempting to view furniture and home decor as a cut-and-paste process, replicating complete rooms in a formulaic way (and often with practically disposable items). Integrating found and collected pieces creates interest in a way that all new furniture just can't accomplish. One client was starting her home from scratch after a devastating fire, having lost not only her house but all the meaningful heirlooms she had collected over the years. As we set out to reestablish her home, we scoured estate sales and antique markets to find one-of-a-kind, timeworn items to make her new home feel rooted in tradition. A walnut secretary from a prestigious auction made its way to her son's bedroom and a rustic farm table anchored an upstairs den. From larger pieces to small, special items, I find truth in the adage, "They just don't make them like they used to."

When choosing furnishings, it's imperative to incorporate some ingenious items that will go the extra mile in a variety of circumstances. Versatile pieces like benches and ottomans are a

Integrated throughout this formal living room are carefully selected antiques. English armchairs are reupholstered in a silk check and gilt frames add a sense of history and luxury.

sneaky seating solution for entertaining large groups. Tuck them under a table to pull out when the need arises. A drop leaf table strategically placed as a sofa table or console will easily give you extra dining space for large groups or holiday hosting. When you think through your needs, you can craft a space with pieces that really function in an intuitive way. This is the luxury of creating a home: you get to tailor it specifically for you and your lifestyle, reinventing even basic items to fit your needs.

Simply put, good basics make a good space. An entry chest can be a gorgeous statement piece but also serves as a functional catchall for mail, stationery, and other odds and ends. Storage ottomans and baskets keep toys and blankets out of sight but accessible. In fact, a roundup of my "go-to" items even led to the beginning of Foundation Goods, a business I started with a dear designer friend to make the foundational items we rely on as designers available in a beautifully curated showroom and online store. In the store, in clients' homes, and in my own home, I turn to these items again and again.

We still have some of our first pieces, including our desk from our first apartment that has lived in my children's rooms and now our home office. My favorite reading chair, now well-worn, has moved from room to room and remains a coveted spot. When a client comes to me with "starter" furniture they have had much longer than they intended, I say, if it's working, keep it! Assess what is worth keeping and invest in custom pieces and well-made antiques to replace the items that are ready for an upgrade. It's the combination of old, new, high, and low that will help you establish a space for the way you want to live.

"Bowood" wallpaper from Colefax and Fowler creates the perfect English cottage backdrop for our client who loves all things British. Strategic pops of color—a vintage rattan mirror painted grass green and a vibrant ceramic lamp—bring life to this room.

OPPOSITE Early on, we knew the sophistication of a marble fireplace would anchor this space. The carvings were hand-drawn and executed perfectly by the mason. **ABOVE** Curated, carefully selected details, whether a wallpapered ceiling, antique mirror, or brightly hued painting, can establish the integrity of a room.

BELOW Wallpaper is an investment, but can instantly establish the identity of a room. In this "dormitory" (my favorite alternative to a traditional bunk room!) cheerful wallpaper acts as an invitation to play. **OPPOSITE** The directives for this boy's room were golf, tennis, and Harry Potter. If you look carefully, you will notice this wallpaper showcases an illustrated set of putters.

MAY THE COURSE
BE WITH YOU

We instantly fell in love with this playful Schumacher wallpaper. Alongside a hanging wicker swing and collection of antique ship mirrors, it brings the right amount of fun to this joyful boy's bedroom.

Style is a way to say who you are
without having to speak.

Rachel Zoe

It takes a brave client to commit to a statement range in a bold color. Though this client generally leans toward elements that are soft and pretty, she fell so in love with this La Cornue range, that we built an entire kitchen around it. To complement the statement piece, we incorporated brass legs on the island and inset brass panels into the bespoke cabinetry by Christopher Scott.

ABOVE In designing this hosting corner, I've mixed practical items with my favorite things: vintage oil paintings, brass candlesticks, and my Grandmother's antique beehive. **OPPOSITE** Cohesively weaving a room together means approaching each different element and layer with the vision of the whole in mind. Here, a palette of neutrals, grays, and creams creates a harmonious conversation between various textural details.

The architecture of this room, with the dynamic ceiling pitch and charming eaves, is a focal point. Balanced by earthy neutrals and raw wood, the effect is both natural and luxurious.

OPPOSITE In more modern spaces, investment pieces often add vitality. The arc of this Danish chair aligns with the curves of the structural arch behind it. **BELOW** This family is full of readers and requested a specific space to accommodate their thoughtful book collection.

This vacation home was developed to be ready for effortless hosting. This table can quickly adapt from dinner to board games, with seats to spare. Though these rush dining chairs are a classic, iconic look, the brass finial distinguishes them.

6

Unify

Incorporate your story and personality through thoughtful selections

SUN VALLEY
HARRISON
NOTABLE BOATS

Once you have established a good foundational base for your room with classic pieces and a functional layout, there is an opportunity to really let your personality shine and tell a story with the next layer. On a recent visit to a friend's home, I instantly recognized pieces of her life—a painting scavenged from a Belgian flea market, souvenirs from a family sabbatical in Denmark, and a bookshelf full of leather-bound Jane Austen novels. I love homes that are personal. I love glimpses of who people love, where they have been, what books they enjoy, and what art they choose.

As a designer, it brings me a lot of satisfaction to be able to help curate and express this perspective in my clients' homes. Through the thoughtful selection of art, photographs, pillows, and accessories, we develop our narrative, which we continue with vintage and heirloom items, souvenirs, and collections. Then we layer in seasonal and transitional elements to keep things fresh. This is when a home really begins to feel lived in and personal as we collect and edit, filling the shelves not just with "things," but with a strong, unified sense of identity. I love meaningful objects not because they are particularly precious or unique, but because they highlight values and memories of the people who live there; they represent the soul of the home. These details give a home a depth that is impossible to accomplish any other way.

Visual unity is first achieved by weaving cohesive threads throughout the home in the form of color, material, or references to a specific style or design element. For one project the formula might be a palette of creamy neutrals and blues, touches of wood and brass, and a reference to something nautical. A navy-striped ottoman with rope trim complements seagrass woven placemats in the kitchen and a coastal painting in the hallway. For another project we might choose sheepskin throws and dimmed lamps for a calming effect. Although each room may showcase a thematic element differently, the fact that these details are incorporated keeps things feeling pulled together from room to room.

The next unifying layer is the personal treasures woven into a home. I recall a client who collected all her daughter's ballet shoes from childhood and lined them up artfully in a large glass vessel. Another client kept vintage door handles from each home they had owned and arranged

With airy linens juxtaposed against rustic wood beams, this primary bedroom at a mountainside home is a welcome retreat. Visual unity is achieved through an earthy color palette and displays of personal treasures. We personalized the space with commissioned paintings of local wildflowers.

them in a lovely bowl adorning her coffee table. Many clients have found a place for a framed family recipe or letter in a mother's or grandmother's handwriting. We have used vintage sports paraphernalia, commissioned art, and antique automobile illustrations that were designed by a grandfather. For my own home I framed my late father-in-law's childhood swimming medals in a simple shadow box as a reminder of a pastime he loved.

With a solid foundation, there is room to incorporate traditions and personality in an evolving way; rearranging a tabletop with a holiday centerpiece, bringing in a new color, or temporarily adding a seasonal plant, scented candle, or piece of art. While I certainly love a "finished" space, I am constantly reinventing and reimagining even my own home. Yes, I do get bored in my own space designed by me! Imagine that! Changing pillows, moving art around, and even sometimes just flipping the chairs from one side of the room to the other for a different view out the window allows me to adapt to and express the mood, the season, and the experiences of my home in simple, subtle, yet creative ways. I also love pieces that can be pulled out and moved around at different times of the year, further "connecting the dots" in a home with meaningful objects that unify the space. If you regularly come to my home, you might observe a slight shift, but rarely are any of the main elements changing.

Curating these personal touches for our clients is like a love letter saying, "We know you. We see you. Look at this beautiful home and life." A stack of curated coffee table books, favorite treats in a strategically placed jar, or a painting of a meaningful place; you can create these "love letters" in your own home! Let these reminders represent and celebrate your best experiences and intentions in order to manifest more.

I don't get to curate art for all our projects, but when I do, we are very conscientious about picking items that connect to the home, the landscape, or our client. In this home a few vintage oil paintings capture familiar scenes from our client's ranch property.

OPPOSITE The suites in this elegant lakeside retreat are designed to grow with the guests. With the addition of a sleeping loft and a two-person bunk room tucked to the side, this room can accommodate a small family. **BELOW** I always like to incorporate something unexpected and playful into a design plan. Here, the energy of the geometric-patterned window seat brings this space to life.

BELOW Throw blankets are a great way to integrate color, texture, and pattern. **OPPOSITE** With the addition of a vintage chair and grouping of antique oil paintings, this formerly plain corner of a large family room is now a memorable moment.

Even a single color interspersed throughout a home can add unity. Here, shades of moody blue are integrated into the cabinetry and on a ceramic lamp.

BELOW Having an accessible, cohesive collection of dishes and serveware makes last minute hosting effortless. **OPPOSITE** With functional open shelving, everyday objects reveal the intention of a space and the personality of those who live there.

eat beautiful
WENDY ROWE
AMANDA BROOKS
FARM FROM HOME
SUNDAY SUPPERS
HEIRLOOM
FOXFIRE LIVING

Great things are not done by impulse,
but a series of small things
brought together.

Vincent Van Gogh

BELOW Perfume is my favorite souvenir to bring home from trips. Here I display my current collection along with some practical containers for storing jewelry. **OPPOSITE** I prefer bathroom tilework to be classic, clean, and timeless. When budget allows, we love to mix slab walls with tilework to create a custom (and easy-to-clean!) look.

ABOVE When we develop a space with a client, we often discuss their daily routines. If we can understand how they want to live, we can understand and incorporate them into the design vision. **OPPOSITE** To complement the pale seaglass cabinetry of this laundry room and break up any heaviness, we introduced a charming cottage element with the addition of a skirt below the sink.

Whirlpool

OPPOSITE The finishing touches of this quaint vignette, such as the brass lamp base, rattan mirror, and blue fabric box, collectively highlight the other design elements in this guest suite. **ABOVE** This antique silver tray showcases some of our client's heirloom jewelry; a commissioned painting stands out among collected objects; framed family photos rest behind a cherished chess set.

This attic-level suite is designed for out-of-town visitors. Cozy nooks like this window seat create individual experiences within a large room. To save guests a trek down to the kitchen if they need a quick bottle of water or treat, we added this petite drink and snack station. Intentionally creating a home means anticipating potential needs and finding creative solutions.

BELOW The stars on this Sister Parish wallpaper introduce a sense of joy. **OPPOSITE** For children's spaces I think it's important to have a playful element, regardless of age. The nautical wallpaper and whimsical bed keep this space from feeling too formal or serious.

Inspired by the Cotswolds, this quaint upstairs bathroom is tucked into the dormers. Featuring many of our client's favorite details, from the antique desk beneath an unexpected modern lamp, to the floral stripe wallpaper, this perfectly proportioned bathroom is reminiscent of a cottage.

7

Inhabit

Savor every
moment at home

The truest purpose of home has never been about a perfect white kitchen or an immaculately organized mudroom. The real meaning of a home comes from the moments we experience within—the dog waiting at the door, splashes in the bathtub, cozy sheets on the bed (that may or may not be "made" quite yet). Some days I look at my home that is lived in and loved by five children and I think to myself, "What happened here?" The answer is Life. Life happened here. Embrace it and be grateful for it.

One of my favorite things to do is tuck my house in at night. In my bustling household, there are many things that need to be "reset" by the end of the day, only to be undone and redone the next. I'm sure you can relate. Once I finish stepping over the toys in the hall, putting away the random papers, and hanging up coats, I am filled with a simple gratitude and satisfaction for what our home is for us and what it provides: a place to gather, connect, retreat, and find respite. I'm sure someday I will miss the dolls on the stairs and the many pairs of shoes by the door, so for now, I try to find the beauty in that instant and recognize that our home is doing its job. After all, homes are meant to be lived in.

It takes a lot of work, heart, and soul to turn a structure into a home and you deserve to enjoy it. Throughout the process of reflecting on what you love, envisioning how you want your home to feel, defining the moments that matter most, creating a solid foundation, establishing purposeful rooms, and unifying everything with meaningful touches, I invite you to give yourself permission to let go and live.

The steps we have taken in this book don't demand linear action; they can be revisited over time. One thing I have loved over the years is revisiting past projects. Whether we are adding another layer, finishing off details, adapting to a changing need, or just refreshing a space, there is something so beautiful about witnessing how a home has changed and how it has stayed the same, marking what has transpired in that space and time and also laying groundwork for the next chapter and aspirations to come.

The impact of a first impression, or in this case, an entrance, should never be underestimated. This space sits at the crossroads of the front yard and connects the gathering room to the rest of the home. It is a room and an experience in itself, but serves as a connecting point.

The real character and identity of a home is evident once you see how people enjoy and use a space and how it supports them. As you embark on this journey of creating a home, I give you permission to unbutton a little, relax, and enjoy things that are perfectly imperfect. This is a process that may at some point feel complete, but it will never be "finished" because the home will grow and evolve with you, just as your needs adapt and shift. Children grow and seasons change. So lean in, live to the fullest, and use your home and the spaces you created for the purposes you envisioned and the space you created. Memories of home stay with us and influence us in unspoken and indelible ways.

One of my memories of the home where I grew up is of a framed piece of art with a playful image and a caption that said, "The rabbit jumped over the moose." To this day I don't know where it came from or what it meant, but I smile when I think of this funny little detail from my childhood. Another memory is the smell of cinnamon, pine, and fresh flowers that takes me back to a friend's home. The tufted leather sofas and silver picture frames could have come straight out of a magazine, but the layer of life and chaos from a family of eleven gave it a sense of unbuttoned formality, making it a joyful, inviting place to be. This home lives in my imagination alongside my other friend's stately house with the baby grand piano. For how they looked and how they felt, the homes in which I spent time clearly left an impression on me.

I strive to channel a feeling in my home where wet feet, grass, and spills aren't a reason to be upset, but a reason to celebrate the life that is happening under my roof. Let's do our best to find the balance between the form and the function, the pretty and the purposeful. Then let's spend our energy on what matters most—the moments we set out to create in the first place. Create a home for a life you love, and the moments will happen, just as you imagined.

OPPOSITE Capturing a place to embrace natural light is a priority in every home. The comfortable furnishings of this "formal" room are an invitation to nap in the glow of late afternoon sunlight. **BELOW** In this primary suite, a streamlined window seat is an ideal location to relax and watch the snow fall.

BELOW A favorite challenge with renovations is to devise how to highlight a home's best features. In this charming, historic property, these arches shine. **OPPOSITE** Wood ceilings, a sculptural light fixture, and a vintage painting add character to this client's mountainside living room.

In a family ranch, wicker, rattan, and raw materials are interspersed throughout each room, from the rattan chandelier in a guest suite, to well-loved straw market bags hung on iron hooks in the foyer.

It always seems to be the extra seats in a room, those tucked beneath a sunlit window, or framing the foot of the bed, that end up being the "spot" everyone loves best.

Basements and game rooms are usually spaces that need to serve many purposes. This multi-functional space is ideal for a busy family.

SMEG

OPPOSITE To bring in the coastal inspiration for this well-traveled mudroom, we leaned on natural materials and a seaside color palette. **BELOW** I stand behind the mindset of "elevating the everyday." Fresh flowers add ambience and bring life and color to a space.

The best rooms have something to say about the people who live in them.

David Hicks

OPPOSITE I strive to design homes which invite our clients to relax and take pause, to rest and reflect. This idyllic bath feels like the pinnacle of that invitation. **ABOVE LEFT** In my home, I display vignettes of personal treasures. Here, an antique brass candlestick sits next to a precious oil painting that reminds me of myself as a child. **ABOVE RIGHT** While certain lighting is designed to fade into the background, light fixtures such as this floral and brass lantern, are designed to shine.

When approaching the design of this kitchen, our client was clear that they wanted something that was purposeful and functional, but also visually stunning and memorable. From the bespoke cabinetry with inset brass panels to the ephemeral color palette, every detail in this kitchen was hand-selected.

Often, it is the way colors harmonize, rather than match that creates cohesion in a space. Here, the pink floral pillow and blue chair reflect the twilight oil paintings across the room.

OPPOSITE Hosting is one of my favorite ways to celebrate the people I love. Sitting down together always feels like a reward. **BELOW** In large family homes, a secondary prep sink is a great use of space.

Living life in your home means using your home. Doing the project, making the mess, cooking the dish. Your home is meant for this. In fact it's even designed for this.

Caitlin's Design Tips

Whether you are designing a lakeside cottage or a family home, here are some tips you can use to elevate your design into something beautiful and intentional.

A LITTLE VINTAGE GOES A LONG WAY.

Rooms that incorporate items with history are so much more interesting and individual than a space where everything came from a catalog or was purchased from a store. Antiques can be incorporated easily through small accessories, art, a chair, end table, or vintage rugs. I love the sense of history and individuality these bring into the design.

DECIDE WHAT IS GOING TO BE THE STAR OF THE SHOW.

Be intentional about your focal point. Whether it's a fireplace, piece of art, or show- stopping sofa, a well-balanced space lets the star shine and allows other pieces to be the supporting cast.

EITHER START WITH THE RUG OR END WITH THE RUG.

Flooring and rugs specifically are one of the largest elements in a space size-wise. Because of this, they contribute a lot to the feel of a space and can sometimes dominate. I've found when planning a space it's easiest to either start with a rug in mind and build off that or develop the other elements and then select a rug at the end that falls in line with the other details and colors that have been selected. Doing it in the middle has never worked out well for me.

DON'T UNDERESTIMATE THE POWER OF A COAT OF PAINT.

A room, a house, or piece of furniture can truly be transformed by giving it new life with paint. Especially if you are on a budget, paint is an affordable way to update your space with maximum impact.

PRIORITIZE QUALITY WHEN PURCHASING HIGH-USE ITEMS.

Items you use every day like a sofa, dining chairs, a bed, and mattress will show the most wear and tear. Investing in durable and comfortable pieces in these areas is key and will save you from having to replace them frequently.

PAY ATTENTION TO COMPETING GEOMETRIES.

My design pet peeve, especially when it comes to tile, trim work, and fabric patterns, is competing geometries. I love an artful mix, but this has to be done carefully. When mixing shapes and patterns, I specifically try to make sure my scale and categories are varied. If you have a trellis, herringbone element, or other geometric pattern, make sure that you balance it with softer, more organic shapes. Too many varied patterns in a space just makes me dizzy!

PLAN YOUR FOUNDATION AND LAYER FROM THERE.

I design rooms in layers. While I start with overall inspiration and a finished look in mind, I make decisions and approach the selections in layers. This makes it easy to pivot or balance elements like color, texture, or materials when adding the next layer. As a team, we generally select all hard finishes attached to the house first, then large furniture elements, then art, accessories, and accents. This allows us to easily change the look down the road or even seasonally just by tweaking elements in the finished layer.

COLORS CAN BE NEUTRAL.

A color used in varying tones and repeatedly in a room can function as a neutral foundation in the space because it is abundant and doesn't stand out. Think about this when making design decisions, especially on large pieces.

MATCHING IS OVERRATED; GO FOR COMPLIMENTARY.

Matching rooms look formulaic and lack depth. Don't worry so much about matching exact colors and elements. Focus on how things balance and coordinate with each other so that the end product is an interesting mix. I will always choose something that complements the existing pieces over something that's an exact match. Anyone can match, but the art is in the mix.

LEAVE ROOM FOR SURPRISE ELEMENTS.

I love elements that feel unexpected. This can translate to a punchy pillow, a dramatic wallpaper or a unique piece of art. The point is that memorable homes are often that way because they have elements that stand out or aren't predictable. Don't be afraid to play around with unexpected details in a way that feels authentic to you.

Acknowledgements

It takes a village to create anything. It is a truly humbling process to consider all the hours, effort and people that contribute to the creation of a home. Each set of hands contributes unique pieces to a project, and the end result is something that supersedes all those individual efforts. Writing this book and building my business have been no different.

I am so grateful for all those who have inspired, supported, and mentored me along the way. What we have created would have been impossible without so many people. I would like to thank all those that have worked as a part of my team over the years. From my very first employee to the team I have now, your energy, efforts, and talents have helped elevate and execute many incredible projects along the way. I have learned from and been inspired by each of your gifts, and I hope I have given you the same experience. I am so proud of what we have accomplished, and I cheer you on as you carve your own paths. I hope as you browse the pages of this book, you see bits and pieces of what we have built together. From items that we've selected, antiques we discovered, fabric we schemed, and many (so many) drawings, these pages are a result of the combined efforts of many people along the way.

I'd like to give a special acknowledgement to my current and recent team who has truly gone the extra mile to help prepare many of our projects specifically for inclusion in this book. We have run fast and hard with amazing opportunities that challenged the limits of our creativity and problem solving. We should feel so proud of the finished result. Megan Garrett, thank you for being my right hand and keeping my head on straight. Lexi Albaraccin, Lauren Swaner and Missy Bledsoe I'm so lucky to have your wit, talent, and work ethic as part of our team. And to my Foundation Goods family, you have taught me so much, and developing the brand with you has been one of the most fulfilling and challenging experiences of my life. I love you all.

We are so lucky to have worked with many incredible architects, builders, and craftsmen that have made our drawings and designs come to life as more than just ideas on a page. The incredible photographers who have captured our work, Rebekah Westover, Lindsey Stewart, and Julia D'Agostino, have found a way to portray the emotion of the layers we have created in such a beautiful way. I love seeing our work through your lens and I love the friendships we have cultivated.

So many clients have trusted us with their homes and dreams and allowed us to bring our added vision to the table. Thank you for giving us the reins and inviting us to bring your dreams into reality. It is a privilege we don't take for granted. The most gratifying part of what we do is to see the life that then inhabits the spaces we have created. I love imagining the memories that are made in your homes.

I feel incredibly lucky to have crossed paths with so many talented people in my industry that have been sounding boards, mentors, and friends. Special thanks to Rochelle Warner, Elizabeth Wixom, and Kimberly Rasmussen, with whom I shared office space for a number of years and from whom I learned so much.

I also feel blessed by my friendships with Bethany Christensen, Marianne Brown, and Steve and Allison Tiek. I feel like we have been on this journey together since the beginning and we have grown so much alongside each other. Bethany, I have so many priceless design memories and experiences that have been shared with you. Thank you for being my buddy on so many market trips and sharing those highs and lows with me. Countless vendors and product reps have helped us curate the perfect selections and taught us about the artistry and craftsmanship of their offerings, supporting our endeavors and solving problems along the way. I have been so lucky to have my team at MLD behind me who have taught me almost everything I know about appliances, plumbing, and hardware and who have supported our team on so many projects.

I have been fortunate to spend time in and live in many meaningful homes in my life. Special thanks to those who have opened your doors to me in every way. Becky and Robb, I love the feeling of coming home and what it feels like to gather with our family. Thank you for the home you gave me, which was not only beautiful but welcoming to everyone. You taught me to always make room for an extra seat at the table. My artist mother and voracious reader of a father have always taught me to look at and explore the world with curious eyes, which has influenced me in meaningful ways.

No one deserves more gratitude than my family and my husband, Dan. You have been supportive and patient with so many stops for errands, detours on vacations to visit a store or to slow drive the neighborhoods, and have been gracious during times when I was occupied by deadlines or duties for work. Ah, the life of a designer. You are talented and inspiring in your own way, and I love nothing more than to support you in your own dreams. Thank you for supporting me in mine.

Special thanks to the dynamic team at Jumelle Press who made this book come to life and committed me to making it happen. Elise and Tiffany, I love that you are not only the publishers of this book, but dear dear friends who I treasure. Your tenacity and vision amaze me, and I am lucky to have you in my circle. I love people who "do things" and you two are the ultimate "doers."

Thank you to Catherine Pavia for her excellent copy editing and writing advice. Also, this physical book wouldn't be what it is without graphic designer Brooke Williams, whose artistic vision and tireless attention to detail brought this book to life.

Of course, this book would not have been possible without my kindred spirit, Britney Mellen, who could download my brain and organize my thoughts in a way that no one else probably could or ever will be able to do. I've loved working alongside you in many different capacities, and my life was made exponentially better the day you moved in up the street.

I am a lucky girl to have found something I love and be given invitations to do it.

BAKE
RORY MACDONALD
THE SILVER SPOON

Credits

Builders

Liesegang Builders, *Rob Liesegang*
Blue Heron Construction, *Dan Davenport*
Neil Whalen Construction, *Neil Whalen*
Killowen Construction, *Tyler Farrell*
Bickmore Construction, *Tony Bickmore*
Tri-City Construction, *Dan Stewart*
Stonybrook Homes, *Kyle Simons*
Lane Myers Construction, *Tyler and Lane Myers*
Gunlock Homes, *Brook Gunlock*
Magleby Construction, *Chad Magleby and Jeff Atkinson*
Northstar Builders, *Tim Gannuscio and Taylor Mulcock*

Photographers

Rebekah Westover
Lindsey Stewart Photography
Julia D'Agostino

Artisans and Services

Antiques and Artisans
Pro Movers, *Sione Otu*
Christopher Scott Cabinetry
Ryan Reeder Cabinets
Benjamin Blackwelder Cabinetry
Smart Millworks, *Phil Klc*
The Finish Guys
Artifacts, *BJan and Becky Djahanbani*
Uptown Drapes, *Geeta Buckley*
Park City Blinds
Classic Upholstery
Sofa Biz
European Expressions

Architects

Highland Group Architecture

Steve Tiek

Clayton Vance Architecture

Lloyd Architecture

Pearson Design Group

MLD

Jodi Nelson

Troy Haney

Jerri Longo

Shay Devenport

Katie Whitehead

Dan and Martina Devenport

Designers

Maddie Waltman

Becca Kamauoha

Lauren Brewer

Kelsey Freestone

Justine Smith

Katie Phelon

Anna Fernandez

Hannah Covey

Courtney Palmer

Lauren Swaner

Missy Bledsoe

Montana Rencher

Morgan Litchfield

Sadie Prince

Jordyn Brasher

Kira McNally

Megan Garrett

Madi Jensen

Lexi Albaraccin

Sienna Harouny

Kayla Brightwell

Aubrey Carlson

Lydia Banks

Olivia Snow

Jamie Millward

Special thanks to

Britney Mellen

Kelsey Winter

Bethany Christensen

Nancy Gleue

Liz Hugentobler

Jenni Johnson

Cammy Fuller

Marcie Busath

Elisa Bulgrin

And our incredible clients who have trusted us with their projects and allowed us to photograph their homes

de Le Cuona
SCHUMACHER
SCHUMACHER

Magnolia Table
THE HOME COOK
BAR TARTINE
TECHNIQUES & RECIPES

MAGNOLIA TABLE
JOANNA GAINES

About the Author

Designer Caitlin Creer is known for her ability to mix function and beauty to create homes that are approachable yet elevated. Since launching her design firm in 2009, Caitlin and her team have envisioned and designed homes across the country, from the mountains to the coasts. Specializing in new construction, luxury vacation properties, and large scale renovations, Caitlin Creer Interiors excels at integrating bespoke details into classical concepts.

In 2020, Caitlin helped launch a lifestyle brand, Foundation Goods, to share curated items that add pretty, yet practical, finishing touches to any space. Showcasing a collection of favorite finds, the brick and mortar location in downtown Salt Lake City has quickly become a beloved shopping destination for both residents and tourists.

When not designing and building homes, Caitlin loves to travel, antique, and have adventures with her husband and five children, who all know their way around a construction site. She lives in Salt Lake City, UT.